ABIDING IN CHRIST

8 STUDIES FOR INDIVIDUALS OR GROUPS

LifeGuide®
BIBLE STUDIES

J. I. PACKER AND CAROLYN NYSTROM

IVP Connect

An imprint of InterVarsity Press
Downers Grove, Illinois

Getting the Most Out of
Abiding in Christ

Of all the Gospel writers, John is the one who works hardest to highlight the divinity of Jesus, God's incarnate Son, and the transforming effects of personal encounter with him, both initial and sustained. This should not surprise us, for John was the closest of the Twelve to Jesus. That is the point he makes by his rather awkward description of himself as "the disciple whom Jesus loved." In some ways, to be sure, Peter, whom Jesus was grooming for leadership, and who was often a spokesman for the Twelve, was closest, but Peter knew that in terms of affectionate intimacy John was ahead of him. So it was John whom Peter asked to find out from Jesus who would betray him (John 13:23-26), as it was John whom Jesus, on the cross, told to look after his mother, Mary (John 19:26-27).

Jesus and John may in fact have been relatives. It is very possible, although not actually provable, that Jesus' mother's sister, and the mother of the sons of Zebedee, and the otherwise unidentified but clearly well-known Salome (John 19:25; Matthew 27:56; Mark 15:40) were the same person, in which case John was Jesus' cousin. Whether this was so or not, John, with his uncannily retentive memory, his spiritually insightful strength of mind, and his simple, profound way of expressing great truths and narrating Jesus' great utterances, is the Gospel writer who excels in presenting the way in which faith-fellowship with the Lord Jesus transforms life. And this is what this set of studies is about.

Abide is an old English word for "remain," "stay steady" and "keep your position." What it means to abide in Christ—that is, always to be resting on him, anchored to him, fixed in him, drawing from him, continually connected and in touch with him—is a pervasive theme in chapters 14—17. There is no more precious lesson to learn, no more enriching link and bond to cherish, no more vital connection to keep snug and tight, so that it never loosens, than this. Abiding in Christ brings peace, joy and love, answers to prayer, and fruitfulness in service. The abiding life is the abundant life.

May these studies be blessed to become a highway into that life.

Suggestions for Individual Study

1. As you begin each study, pray that God will speak to you through his Word.

2. Read the introduction to the study and respond to the personal reflection question or exercise. This is designed to help you focus on God and on the theme of the study.

3. Each study deals with a particular passage so that you can delve into the author's meaning in that context. Read and reread the passage to be studied. The questions are written using the language of the New International Version, so you may wish to use that version of the Bible. The New Revised Standard Version is also recommended.

4. This is an inductive Bible study, designed to help you discover for yourself what Scripture is saying. The study includes three types of questions. *Observation* questions ask about the basic facts: who, what, when, where and how. *Interpretation* questions delve into the meaning of the passage. *Application* questions help you discover the implications of the text for growing in Christ. These three keys unlock the treasures of Scripture.

Write your answers to the questions in the spaces provided

or in a personal journal. Writing can bring clarity and deeper understanding of yourself and of God's Word.

5. It might be good to have a Bible dictionary handy. Use it to look up any unfamiliar words, names or places.

6. Use the prayer suggestion to guide you in thanking God for what you have learned and to pray about the applications that have come to mind.

7. You may want to go on to the suggestion under "Now or Later," or you may want to use that idea for your next study.

Suggestions for Members of a Group Study

1. Come to the study prepared. Follow the suggestions for individual study mentioned above. You will find that careful preparation will greatly enrich your time spent in group discussion.

2. Be willing to participate in the discussion. The leader of your group will not be lecturing. Instead, he or she will be encouraging the members of the group to discuss what they have learned. The leader will be asking the questions that are found in this guide.

3. Stick to the topic being discussed. Your answers should be based on the verses which are the focus of the discussion and not on outside authorities such as commentaries or speakers. These studies focus on a particular passage of Scripture. Only rarely should you refer to other portions of the Bible. This allows for everyone to participate in in-depth study on equal ground.

4. Be sensitive to the other members of the group. Listen attentively when they describe what they have learned. You may be surprised by their insights! Each question assumes a variety of answers. Many questions do not have "right" answers, particularly questions that aim at meaning or application. Instead the questions push us to explore the passage more thoroughly.

When possible, link what you say to the comments of others.

Also, be affirming whenever you can. This will encourage some of the more hesitant members of the group to participate.

5. Be careful not to dominate the discussion. We are sometimes so eager to express our thoughts that we leave too little opportunity for others to respond. By all means participate! But allow others to also.

6. Expect God to teach you through the passage being discussed and through the other members of the group. Pray that you will have an enjoyable and profitable time together, but also that as a result of the study you will find ways that you can take action individually and/or as a group.

7. Remember that anything said in the group is considered confidential and should not be discussed outside the group unless specific permission is given to do so.

8. If you are the group leader, you will find additional suggestions at the back of the guide.

1

A Life of Love

The great religions had founders, and the founders had disciples. But none evoked such awe, affection and loyalty in his disciples (even despite bewilderment) as did Jesus Christ, the God-Man.

Bafflement breaks surface as Jesus talks to them before his betrayal. What does it mean for God to glorify himself in Christ and Christ in himself? What does it mean that the Spirit, Father and Son will be with and in them together, in revelatory action? All that is beyond them, as their questions show.

But Jesus is directing them to a life of loving him and each other, of looking longingly for him to take them to his home, and of listening to his words so as to learn more—and he's teaching them that life could begin there and then. Today he calls us to the same life pattern, starting from where we are here and now. Will we say yes?

GROUP DISCUSSION. When, how and why have you stayed close to someone even when separated by distance?

PERSONAL REFLECTION. Who has loved you at a time when love was difficult? How have you been impacted by that love? Thank God for it.

It is Jesus' last evening with his disciples. He has washed their feet and told them to serve one another in a similar way; he has instituted the sacrament of Communion with bread and cup, proclaiming it as his own body and blood; and he has announced that one of them will betray him that very night. Judas immediately left the table. *Read John 13:31—14:4.*

1. If you had been an unseen observer during this whole evening, what questions would you have wanted to ask after the dialogue of these verses?

2. "Do not let your hearts be troubled," says Jesus at the end of his announcement of upcoming events. Why might the disciples need that admonition at this point?

3. Peter asks two questions in this scene. How might the answers he receives bring both comfort and alarm?

4. With your own perspective of this scene today, what can you understand about Jesus' answers that Peter might not yet have understood?

5. Immediately after Judas left the room, Jesus uses the words *glorify* or *glorified* five times (13:31-32). Once again using your hindsight, what all can you now see that Jesus meant by "glorify" and "glorified"?

6. Of all the final commands Jesus might have left with his followers, why do you think he now says, "Love one another"?

When have you been the beneficiary of this command?

7. Jesus describes the love his followers are to cultivate by saying, "As I have loved you, so you must love one another" (v. 34). Think back over what you know of the life of Jesus. What scenes of love stand out in your mind?

8. How is Jesus' promise in verses 14:2-4 an expression of his love for his followers?

9. Consider one relationship where love is difficult for you. If you were going to love this person as Christ has loved you, what would you begin to do—and not do?

10. Jesus continues his description of love by pointing to a result or purpose: "By this all men will know that you are my disciples, if you love one another" (13:35). What does this statement suggest about the goal of Jesus' ministry and about what the impact of it will be?

11. Consider the cluster of "disciples" to which you belong and prayerfully reread Jesus' "new command" of 13:34. What needs to happen in your cluster of Christ-followers for you to fully meet this command?

Thank God for the good work that he is doing among and through your community. Ask him to bring about any needed change.

Now or Later

Jesus told his disciples, "In my Father's house are many rooms;
. . . I am going there to prepare a place for you." If you belong to
Jesus, he makes the same promise to you. Take time to explore
your thoughts and feelings about heaven. Compose a painting,
poem or song that expresses some of these ideas. Use it as a
prayer to Jesus.

2

Which Way to God?

Since Jesus has already identified himself as the bread of life (John 6) and the gate (John 10:7-10) and shepherd of God's sheep (John 10:11-18), it should not surprise us when he calls himself the *way* (to a personal, parent-child relationship with God), the *truth* (ultimate reality, and final standard for all talk about God) and the *life* (who makes it possible for us to live the abundant life God desires for us now and eternally).

God's perfect Fatherhood implies constant love, thoughtful care, powerful protection, ongoing instruction, wise guidance and a nurturing strategy that prepares us to be at home with him and Jesus in heaven forever. Coming to him and knowing him means going beyond awareness of his reality to enter the fullness of this relationship. Penitent faith in Jesus as sin-bearing Savior and reigning Lord brings us into it.

The Father exalts his Son by making him central at every stage in the work of our salvation. These are deep and wonderful waters.

GROUP DISCUSSION. In our world today people are looking for God in many different places. What paths to God do you see people exploring?

PERSONAL REFLECTION. Reflect on your faith commitments.

Why do you remain in the faith?

We continue to follow Jesus' last conversation with his disciples where he announces that he is leaving, and his startled friends ask questions. In this section he responds to Thomas and then Philip. *Read John 14:5-14.*

1. Philip asks Jesus, "Lord, show us the Father and that will be enough for us." What connections throughout this passage does Jesus draw between himself and God the Father?

2. What connections do you see between Philip's request and Thomas' question (vv. 5-8)?

3. Focus on Jesus' bold statement of verse 6. If the disciples gathered around him would fully accept this statement, what impact would it have on them in this difficult time?

4. Why is Jesus' statement of verse 6 offensive to many people today?

Do you find his statement challenging? troubling? comforting? confusing? Why or why not?

---

5. In reply to Philip's request Jesus says, "Anyone who has seen me has seen the Father." What does this hint about the nature of God?

---

6. In verse 12 Jesus says, "Anyone who has faith in me will do what I have been doing." Mentally review your plans for the coming week. What personal challenge do you find in Jesus' statement?

---

7. With hindsight on two thousand years of Christianity throughout the world, what do you think Jesus means in verse 12 when he says, "He will do even greater things than these"?

8. Focus on verses 13-14. First give these two sentences a quick reading as if you were seeing them for the first time. What would be your first response?

9. Now read these same two sentences slowly, noting small phrases such as "so that" and "in my name." With these conditions in mind, what specifically do you now want to ask Jesus to do?

10. Meditate silently for a few moments on the words of Jesus in verse 6: "I am the way and the truth and the life. No one comes to the Father except through me." Consider the kinds of comments made by your friends or heard in the media about Christians' belief that Christ is the only way to God. How can you respond?

As you weigh the impact of this bold statement from Jesus, pray for those you know who have not yet recognized him as their Lord, and pray for your own part in their spiritual care.

Now or Later

Look for an opportunity this week to engage in meaningful conversation with a person who is on a totally different "God path" than your own.

3

Looking Within

Just when devout Jews were beginning to see a human (Jesus) somehow embody the divine as Yahweh's Son, Jesus introduces a greater confusion: God is also Spirit, the *Holy* Spirit—which sent the rabbis digging for a fresh look at their Hebrew texts. So here, now, is the truth of the Trinity—three identical persons within one divine being and life, all bonded together in love, and all involved in everything that each does: the Father being the planner, the Son his agent and the Holy Spirit the executive of both. This is our God!

The Spirit indwelling Christ's servants makes us aware that the Father and the Son, who lives in us, are actually with us. Our inner life is supernaturalized, and we find ourselves alive in the Lord.

GROUP DISCUSSION. When getting to know someone, does looking beneath the surface come naturally to you, or are you more likely to know a person by what they say and do? Describe an example of this from your experience.

PERSONAL REFLECTION. If someone were to know you "from the inside out" what would they likely discover?

Having identified himself as intricately connected with God the Father, Jesus now introduces the third person of the Trinity: the Holy Spirit. But to know the Spirit, we must look within. *Read John 14:15-31.*

1. This section of Jesus' talk with his disciples is like a "quote book" of famous sayings of Jesus. Which saying here do you find particularly meaningful? Why?

2. Find each mention of the Holy Spirit in this passage. What all can you know about him from these citations?

3. Jesus continues to link himself with the Father as he did in the previous reading. What further development of this connection do you find here?

4. Throughout these descriptions of connection between Father, Son and Spirit, Jesus also speaks of his followers. Where do you find yourself in the text of these various connections?

Stop for a moment and pray about what this means to you.

---

5. What connections do you find between obedience and love in this text?

In view of these connections, what do you think would happen if a person tried to love God but did not try to obey him?

---

6. Jesus comforts his disciples about his coming death by saying, "I will not leave you as orphans; I will come to you" (v. 18). In view of Jesus' various statements before and after this important promise, what all do you think Jesus means by these words? (Examine verses 16-21.)

7. Verse 20 says, "On that day you will realize that . . . I am in you" (v. 20). As you consider this whole section of Jesus' teaching, what evidence would you hope to find if you looked within yourself in search of the presence of Christ?

---

8. "But, Lord, why do you intend to show yourself to us and not to the world?" asks the other Judas (v. 22). As you reexamine Jesus' full response to that question (vv. 23-31), what all can you say about Jesus' desires for his disciples?

for the world?

---

9. Jesus says to his disciples (and to us), "Because I live, you also will live" (v. 19). What does Jesus mean by this statement?

How can you reflect this statement as you go about your current activities in the world?

10. Jesus draws their time together in the upper room to a close in much the same way that he began: "Do not let your hearts be troubled" (vv. 1, 27). Slowly read aloud the words of verse 27 as though Jesus is now speaking them to you. In what areas of your life do you most need, and now receive, this blessing of peace?

Pray, thanking God for the stability he brings to these troubled areas.

Now or Later

On a large piece of paper, combine your artistic and your linguistic skills by drawing a design of the Trinity relationship defined in this chapter. Experiment with classic artistic expressions such as a triangle or interconnected circles as you create symbols linking Father, Son and Spirit. Draw lines of connection and label each line with phrases from John 14. Study the resulting annotated illustration as you attempt to better comprehend the nature of our triune God.

4

Being Connected

John 15:1-17

For those who train dogs in obedience, "Stay!" is a key command. It requires the dog to stand still, "stay put" and not change its position, for as long as the trainer wishes. This takes discipline on the dog's part; some never learn to do it, even after years of training.

Jesus tells Christians to "stay put" in him—that is, to maintain dependence on him for vision, goodwill and wisdom to act, and help as they act. He compares this connection to a branch of a vine, drawing nourishment from the main stem, because as vintners want many grapes on their vines, so the Father and the Son want much fruit from our lives—effective influence in works of love that witness to who Christ is and help bring the kingdom of God to earth.

"Without me you can do nothing," warns Jesus. Hasty, self-reliant people find this a hard lesson to learn. But learn it we must, if our lives are to please and honor our Lord.

GROUP DISCUSSION. Would you say that you are a "natural connector" or a "natural loner"? How does this natural preference show up in your choices?

PERSONAL REFLECTION. Reflect on your natural inclination to either connect with other people or to be alone. If you are a natural loner, what do you need to overcome in order to make important connections with others? If you are a natural connector, what do you need to overcome in order to have fruitful time alone?

At the close of chapter 14, Jesus said to his disciples, "Come now; let us leave." Leave to go where? They are likely now walking together the road toward Gethsemane, but Jesus continues their conversation. *Read John 15:1-17.*

1. In this passage, Jesus continues to speak of truths he introduced earlier during this last conversation with his disciples, and he also interjects some new ideas. What do you find here that is familiar, and what do you find that is new?

2. What is revealed about the relationship between God and his people as you study Jesus' image of the vine (vv. 1-8)?

3. Notice that several times Jesus uses the word *remain* (NIV) as he speaks of life on the vine. What cautions and what encouragements do you find as you study his various uses of that word?

4. When and how have you experienced the connectedness of life on the vine?

5. Jesus' image of life on the vine includes happy words like *fruit* and painful words like *prunes,* but all within the context that "no branch can bear fruit by itself" (v. 4). When have you seen the value of both pruning and fruitfulness in your own section of God's vine?

6. Focus on verses 9-16. As you notice various uses of the word *love* in these verses, what all can you know about the kind of love that God gives and expects?

7. What does it mean to "remain in love"?

8. What is the difference between a servant and a friend (vv. 13-15)?

9. What are the privileges of being a friend of Jesus?

10. Why do you think Jesus uses the phrases "I have called you" and "I chose you"?

11. "This is my command: Love each other," says Jesus in verse 17. As you consider again the metaphor of the vine, why is the presence or absence of love so important?

12. Mentally take stock of your own place among the branches of Jesus, the vine. How are you giving and receiving love?

The vine of Christ stretches throughout the world with branches reaching in all directions. Pray for one area of that branch system that you know is currently troubled.

Now or Later

Pencil-sketch a vine with many interconnecting branches. Highlight your section of the branches as they connect to the vine. Mark those branches with names of people and ministries and sketch your various connections to each. Include any "fruit" that you are aware of. Consider various weaknesses and strengths in your drawing of branches and revise the shape and size of the branches accordingly. Show the centrality of the vine and the various interwoven connections of the branches. Prayerfully reflect on what your pencil-sketch reveals.

5

Overcoming Rejection

Rejection, for whatever reason, always hurts. Often it makes us want to run away, as this line from an old poem captures: "I turned and fled; I could not face humiliation and disgrace." Christ's gospel, entrusted to us, invades people's comfort zones and challenges their pride, and so guarantees profound hostility and frequent rejection. Satan, too, in his unending cosmic battle with God, constantly stirs up opposition to Christians and their message. So witnessing believers must expect trouble and disheartening feelings.

But not only trouble; triumph, as well! For the Spirit witnesses through us, convincing people deep down that Christ was righteous and right in everything, that unbelief is sin, and that Satan, for all his rampaging, is already a condemned, defeated foe. So conversions will happen, God's kingdom will advance, and through all the conflict Christ will be glorified.

Stand steady, then, and keep on keeping on!

GROUP DISCUSSION. What are some subtle or not so subtle ways that people reject one another?

PERSONAL REFLECTION. Would you say that you have a thick or

thin skin when it comes to rejection? Reflect on what this might show about your concept of self and how you experience security.

While much of Jesus' last conversation with his disciples up to this point has focused on comfort and encouragement, he did not want his disciples to enter the next phase of their ministry unprepared. Life was going to get hard—and soon. *Read John 15:18—16:16.*

1. What hardships could the disciples expect according to this passage?

2. Why will people reject Jesus' disciples (15:18—16:4)?

3. Jesus says, "All this I have told you so that you will not go astray" (16:1). If you had been among those early eleven disciples, do you think you would have had enough information here to endure what lies ahead? Why or why not?

4. Jesus says of their future persecutors, "If I had not come and spoken to them, they would not be guilty of sin. Now, however, they have no excuse for their sin" (15:22). How do you interpret this rather strange statement?

5. In view of the kind of reception Jesus tells his disciples to expect, why do you think he still tells them, "You also must testify [about me]" (15:27)?

6. In what ways can you expect to participate in the rejection described here—and also in the mission assigned?

7. Even though Jesus promises his disciples much hardship ahead, he also offers help. What various forms of help do you find in 16:5-16?

8. Jesus says that when the Holy Spirit comes he will convict the world of sin, righteousness and judgment (16:8). Of what value would it be to an unbeliever to be convicted of sin, righteousness and judgment?

9. What work does Jesus say the Holy Spirit will do among Christ-followers (16:12-15)?

10. Jesus describes a cosmic battle in this section of John. Where do you see yourself in this scene?

What do you hope from yourself?

from God?

If you are able, pray, asking God to place you in the front lines of his cosmic battle. Ask also for enough vision of the spiritual cosmic scene to endure rejection when necessary, and to persevere in a faithful telling of the good news of Jesus.

Now or Later

Many Christians around the world experience severe suffering because of their faith in Jesus. This week begin a deliberate participation with them. Actions to consider:

- Write a letter of encouragement to a spiritual brother or sister who lives in an area where practicing the Christian faith is a difficult challenge.

- Send a message to an authority in an oppressive government, or to one of your own political leaders, urging them to exert influence for spiritual freedom.

- Begin to read and pray your way around the world one country at a time by using a resource such as *Operation World.**

---

*Patrick Johnston and Jason Mandryk, *Operation World: When We Pray God Works* (London: Paternoster Lifestyle, 2001).

6

Anticipating the Future

John 16:16-33

Human beings live very much in their future; things that we expect to happen affect us right now. Christ teaches us to foresee endless joy with himself, and tells us that keeping this prospect on our minds will give us present peace and strengthen us to work through whatever spells of grief may come our way.

For Christians, the future is guaranteed to be better than the past ever was, or the present now is. The best is yet to be. The famous tag line "You ain't seen nothing yet" is always a word in season for the servants of Jesus.

GROUP DISCUSSION. What would you like to know (and not know) about the future? Why?

PERSONAL REFLECTION. When you consider the future, either in this life or eternity, what is your general feeling? Apprehension? Anticipation? Joy? Fear? Worry? Frustration? Contentment? Challenge? Trust? Some mixture of . . . ? Why? How do your feelings about the future connect (or not connect) with your relationship to Christ?

Today's Scripture passage is Jesus' final words of teaching to his disciples prior to his death. (The remainder of this "Farewell Address" is a prayer—to God.) Not surprisingly, Jesus asks his disciples to look ahead. *Read John 16:16-33.*

---

1. This dialogue contains several shifts in mood. If you had been part of this scene, what would you have been feeling at various points of the conversation? Why?

---

2. What events do you think Jesus has in mind when he tells his disciples to prepare for both joy and grief in their immediate future (vv. 16-22)?

Does joy or grief seem most important in this text? Why?

---

3. Jesus says, "You will weep and mourn while the world rejoices" (v. 20). Do you think the disciples are surprised by this statement from Jesus? Why or why not? (Review 15:18—16:4.)

---

4. Jesus says that "no one will take away your joy" (v. 22). Does this mean they will never be sad again? Why or why not?

5. How is Jesus' coming death and resurrection in some ways like childbirth?

6. For the fourth time in this conversation, Jesus speaks of powerful praying (v. 23). How does his coming death and resurrection change the relationship between the disciples and God (vv. 23-28)?

7. "The Father himself loves you because you have loved me and have believed that I came from God." Do you believe that Jesus could say these same words about you? If so, mentally skip back through your past twenty-four hours, and play it again in slow motion, imagining in each scene that you are sheltered by the phrase "Loved by God." What do you see, hear, think, feel as you review these scenes?

8. "You believe at last!" shouts Jesus near the end of their conversation (v. 31). How would these words and the rest of his closing statements help his disciples keep on believing through and beyond the difficult days ahead (vv. 29-33)?

9. What kinds of faith support has God provided you in your own difficult days?

---

10. Take a look at your future: near future, far future, eternal future. How do the words of verse 33 affect your plans, thoughts and feelings about your future?

When you think of your future, what feelings are likely to rise? Hope? Anticipation? Fear? Worry? Dread? Confidence? Bring these feelings (both positive and negative) to your loving Lord.

Now or Later

Write out the words of John 16:33 in the space below. Meditate on each phrase, looking for ways that it touches your own life. These words are as much for Christ-followers today as they were for his first disciples. Respond in prayer.

7

Defining Purpose

To know that your adored leader prays for you can be an overwhelming discovery of committed love. Surely the Eleven were overwhelmed when their Master turned from talking *to them*—at length and with feeling—about the Father, to talking, still at length and with feeling, *to the Father* about them. Knowing he must leave them behind in a perverse and corrupt world, he asks for their continued protection from Satan, their sworn enemy for their ongoing holiness and sanctification; for lasting unity with each other, as proof of their new supernatural life; and for them finally to be with him in his glory beyond this world. Clearly, Jesus wants them to overhear his prayer so as to realize that his love for them is not going to fade, but is an eternal reality.

Shouldn't we be equally overwhelmed to know that from this throne Jesus intercedes for us in exactly these terms? Discipleship takes wings when we constantly remind ourselves that *at this moment Jesus, my Savior, Lord and Friend, is praying for me.*

GROUP DISCUSSION. If you were setting out on a complex mission or task, what would be most important for you to know?

PERSONAL REFLECTION. Suppose you were able to say to God at the end of your life, "I have completed the work you gave me to do." What would you want that to mean?

Four times during his goodbye conversation with his disciples, Jesus admonishes them to pray, and each time he makes powerful promises connected with prayer. Now at the end, Jesus prays in their presence: first for himself, then for his followers. *Read John 17:1-19.*

---

1. Focus particularly on Jesus' prayer for himself in verses 1-5. What do you learn here about Christ and his purpose?

---

2. Several times in his prayer for himself, Jesus uses words and phrases that speak of time. What does his use of time language reveal to you about time and eternity, God and his people?

---

3. How can Jesus' prayer for himself contribute to your own worship of God as Trinity?

---

4. "I pray for them," says Jesus in verse 9. At this point in his ministry Jesus has eleven remaining disciples: Peter, James (son of Zebedee), John, Andrew, Philip, Bartholomew, Matthew, Thomas, James (son of Alphaeus), Thaddaeus, Simon. Select one of these disciples as your own "stand-in," and for the moment give yourself one of these names. Read verses 6-19, listening to Jesus' prayer through the ears of this disciple with all that you imagine him to be. What words and phrases are important to this disciple you have chosen to imitate? Why?

Which words and phrases are important to you in your own context? Why?

5. Review uses of the term *world*, which Jesus uses nearly a dozen times in this prayer. What good can Christ-followers accomplish because they are *in* the world, but not *of* the world?

6. Read again this petition in Jesus' prayer: "Holy Father, protect them by the power of your name—the name you gave me—so that they may be one as we are one" (v. 11). In view of the task and the purpose that Jesus has given his followers, why is the kind of unity described here important?

7. When and how have you experienced this kind of kinship with other believers?

8. Prayerfully read the last three sentences of Jesus' prayer for his disciples (vv. 17-19). What does this second part of Jesus' prayer in John 17 suggest about his purpose—and its impact on his followers?

9. Jesus began this prayer for his disciples with a statement to his Father: "I have revealed you to those whom you gave me out of the world" (v. 6). As you think back over what you know of Jesus' life and teachings, when and how have you seen Jesus reveal the true nature of his Father?

10. When have you seen God revealed in or through someone?

11. Mentally picture a dozen people who follow you in one way or another. What would have to happen for you to be able to say at the end of your life, "Father, I have revealed you to those whom you gave me out of the world"?

Spend some time in prayer thanking God for these early disciples and Jesus' ministry through them.

Now or Later

Select one of the eleven disciples who remained with Jesus at this point. Research how that person spent the remainder of his life. Consider ways that this disciple lived out the purposes expressed in Jesus' prayer for him.

8

Leaving a Legacy

When Jesus prayed for the whole church, he divided it into two classes: the original disciples, who became apostles, whose message became the New Testament (the rule of Christian faith); and everyone else, "those who will believe in me through their message"—including, of course, ourselves.

God the Father gave to his Son all Christians (past, present and future) to love and to save. He called us all to be one (together) transculturally, transglobally and transhistorically. We are to live out that bond in faith, love, holiness and mission; these are the unchanging realities of our life together. But we do not attempt this kind of spiritual togetherness without help. God himself created a model and so allows us a glimpse of the active bond between Father and Son during the Son's earthly ministry. All Christians share the destiny of contemplating and being enriched by the Son in his glory forever and ever.

These are the certainties and fixed points by which we should be living as Christ's disciples in church today.

GROUP DISCUSSION. Suppose you could drop in on your church one hundred years from now. What would you hope to find?

PERSONAL REFLECTION. If you were praying for your great-great grandchildren, what would you ask God for?

In the final words of Jesus' farewell, he continues to pray—this time for his followers of the distant future. *Read John 17:20-26.*

1. As you picture Jesus speaking the words of this prayer to his Father on your behalf, what do you find particularly compelling?

2. What part does love have in this prayer?

3. What times and places does Jesus' prayer here encompass?

What do these reveal about God?

about all who believe in Jesus?

4. How would you describe the unity mentioned in these verses?

5. What are some of your most powerful experiences of unity with other believers?

6. Where and how do you see troubling forms of disunity between God's people?

7. What gifts does Jesus ask God to give you in this prayer?

8. What seems to be the purpose of this lavish legacy?

9. As you consider your place among the people of God, what can you do to promote the kind of unity that Jesus prays for?

10. Jesus prayed for you, "May [insert your name here] also be in us so that the world may believe . . ." How can you begin or continue to live out that legacy?

Read aloud Jesus' prayer for you as recorded in verses 20-26. Then pray your response in return.

Now or Later

Echo the prayer of Jesus by praying his words for a church or ministry that seems to need the blessings described in his prayer for all future believers. Pause now and then to pray for specific needs and people in that organization.

Leader's Notes

Leading a Bible discussion can be an enjoyable and rewarding experience. But it can also be *scary*—especially if you've never done it before. If this is your feeling, you're in good company. When God asked Moses to lead the Israelites out of Egypt, he replied, "O Lord, please send someone else to do it!" (Ex 4:13). It was the same with Solomon, Jeremiah and Timothy, but God helped these people in spite of their weaknesses, and he will help you as well.

You don't need to be an expert on the Bible or a trained teacher to lead a Bible discussion. The idea behind these inductive studies is that the leader guides group members to discover for themselves what the Bible has to say. This method of learning will allow group members to remember much more of what is said than a lecture would.

These studies are designed to be led easily. As a matter of fact, the flow of questions through the passage from observation to interpretation to application is so natural that you may feel that the studies lead themselves. This study guide is also flexible. You can use it with a variety of groups—student, professional, neighborhood or church groups. Each study takes forty-five to sixty minutes in a group setting.

There are some important facts to know about group dynamics and encouraging discussion. The suggestions listed below should enable you to effectively and enjoyably fulfill your role as leader.

Preparing for the Study

1. Ask God to help you understand and apply the passage in your own life. Unless this happens, you will not be prepared to lead others. Pray too for the various members of the group. Ask God to open your hearts to the message of his Word and motivate you to action.

2. Read the introduction to the entire guide to get an overview of the entire book and the issues which will be explored.

3. As you begin each study, read and reread the assigned Bible passage to familiarize yourself with it.

4. This study guide is based on the New International Version of the Bible. It will help you and the group if you use this translation as the basis for your study and discussion.

5. Carefully work through each question in the study. Spend time in meditation and reflection as you consider how to respond.

6. Write your thoughts and responses in the space provided in the study guide. This will help you to express your understanding of the passage clearly.

7. It might help to have a Bible dictionary handy. Use it to look up any unfamiliar words, names or places. (For additional help on how to study a passage, see chapter five of *How to Lead a LifeGuide Bible Study*, InterVarsity Press.)

8. Consider how you can apply the Scripture to your life. Remember that the group will follow your lead in responding to the studies. They will not go any deeper than you do.

9. Once you have finished your own study of the passage, familiarize yourself with the leader's notes for the study you are leading. These are designed to help you in several ways. First, they tell you the purpose the study guide author had in mind when writing the study. Take time to think through how the study questions work together to accomplish that purpose. Second, the notes provide you with additional background information or suggestions on group dynamics for various questions. This information can be useful when people have difficulty understanding or answering a question. Third, the leader's notes can alert you to potential problems you may encounter during the study.

10. If you wish to remind yourself of anything mentioned in the leader's notes, make a note to yourself below that question in the study.

Leading the Study

1. Begin the study on time. Open with prayer, asking God to help the group to understand and apply the passage.

2. Be sure that everyone in your group has a study guide. Encourage the group to prepare beforehand for each discussion by reading the introduction to the guide and by working through the questions in the study.

3. At the beginning of your first time together, explain that these studies are meant to be discussions, not lectures. Encourage the members of the group to participate. However, do not put pressure on those who may be hesitant to speak during the first few sessions. You may want to suggest the following guidelines to your group.

☐ Stick to the topic being discussed.

☐ Your responses should be based on the verses which are the focus of the discussion and not on outside authorities such as commentaries or speakers.

☐ These studies focus on a particular passage of Scripture. Only rarely should you refer to other portions of the Bible. This allows for everyone to participate in in-depth study on equal ground.

☐ Anything said in the group is considered confidential and will not be discussed outside the group unless specific permission is given to do so.

☐ We will listen attentively to each other and provide time for each person present to talk.

☐ We will pray for each other.

4. Have a group member read the introduction at the beginning of the discussion.

5. Every session begins with a group discussion question. The question or activity is meant to be used before the passage is read. The question introduces the theme of the study and encourages group members to begin to open up. Encourage as many members as possible to participate, and be ready to get the discussion going with your own response.

This section is designed to reveal where our thoughts or feelings need to be transformed by Scripture. That is why it is especially important not to read the passage before the discussion question is asked. The passage will tend to color the honest reactions people would otherwise give because they are, of course, supposed to think the way the Bible does.

You may want to supplement the group discussion question with an icebreaker to help people to get comfortable. See the community section of *Small Group Idea Book* for more ideas.

You also might want to use the personal reflection question with your group. Either allow a time of silence for people to respond individually or discuss it together.

6. Have a group member (or members if the passage is long) read aloud the passage to be studied. Then give people several minutes to read the passage again silently so that they can take it all in.

7. Question 1 will generally be an overview question designed to briefly survey the passage. Encourage the group to look at the whole passage, but try to avoid getting sidetracked by questions or issues that will be addressed later in the study.

8. As you ask the questions, keep in mind that they are designed to be used just as they are written. You may simply read them aloud. Or you may prefer to express them in your own words.

There may be times when it is appropriate to deviate from the study guide. For example, a question may have already been answered. If so, move on to the next question. Or someone may raise an important question not covered in the guide. Take time to discuss it, but try to keep the group from going off on tangents.

9. Avoid answering your own questions. If necessary, repeat or rephrase them until they are clearly understood. Or point out something you read in the leader's notes to clarify the context or meaning. An eager group quickly becomes passive and silent if they think the leader will do most of the talking.

10. Don't be afraid of silence. People may need time to think about the question before formulating their answers.

11. Don't be content with just one answer. Ask, "What do the rest of you think?" or "Anything else?" until several people have given answers to the question.

12. Acknowledge all contributions. Try to be affirming whenever possible. Never reject an answer. If it is clearly off-base, ask, "Which verse led you to that conclusion?" or again, "What do the rest of you think?"

13. Don't expect every answer to be addressed to you, even though this will probably happen at first. As group members become more at ease, they will begin to truly interact with each other. This is one sign of healthy discussion.

14. Don't be afraid of controversy. It can be very stimulating. If you don't resolve an issue completely, don't be frustrated. Move on and keep it in mind for later. A subsequent study may solve the problem.

15. Periodically summarize what the group has said about the passage. This helps to draw together the various ideas mentioned and gives continuity to the study. But don't preach.

16. At the end of the Bible discussion you may want to allow group members a time of quiet to work on an idea under "Now or Later." Then discuss what you experienced. Or you may want to encourage group members to work on these ideas between meetings. Give an opportunity

during the session for people to talk about what they are learning.

17. Conclude your time together with conversational prayer, adapting the prayer suggestion at the end of the study to your group. Ask for God's help in following through on the commitments you've made.

18. End on time.

Many more suggestions and helps are found in *How to Lead a LifeGuide Bible Study.*

Components of Small Groups

A healthy small group should do more than study the Bible. There are four components to consider as you structure your time together.

Nurture. Small groups help us to grow in our knowledge and love of God. Bible study is the key to making this happen and is the foundation of your small group.

Community. Small groups are a great place to develop deep friendships with other Christians. Allow time for informal interaction before and after each study. Plan activities and games that will help you get to know each other. Spend time having fun together going on a picnic or cooking dinner together.

Worship and prayer. Your study will be enhanced by spending time praising God together in prayer or song. Pray for each other's needs and keep track of how God is answering prayer in your group. Ask God to help you to apply what you are learning in your study.

Outreach. Reaching out to others can be a practical way of applying what you are learning, and it will keep your group from becoming self-focused. Host a series of evangelistic discussions for your friends or neighbors. Clean up the yard of an elderly friend. Serve at a soup kitchen together, or spend a day working on a Habitat house.

Many more suggestions and helps in each of these areas are found in *Small Group Idea Book.* Information on building a small group can be found in *Small Group Leaders' Handbook* and *The Big Book on Small Groups* (both from InterVarsity Press). Reading through one of these books would be worth your time.

Study 1. A Life of Love. John 13:31—14:4.

Purpose: To know the love of Jesus and extend a similar love to others.

Question 1. With our twentieth-century hindsight through two thousand years of Christianity, it's hard to imagine the shocking improbability of almost every phrase of this dialogue. Invite your group to put themselves behind the first-century draperies of this room and wonder such questions as: Where did Judas go? Why? Why does Jesus link his death with glory? What is the relationship between God and Jesus? Did God have a son? Who? How? Is that blasphemy? Where is Jesus going? Why does he want his disciples to love each other? Why does he want people to know that these are his disciples? Why is love important? What kind of love? How would they show it? Why can't Peter follow Jesus now? What did Jesus mean when he said Peter would follow him later? What is going to happen tonight that would change Peter so much? Why shouldn't the disciples be troubled? Wouldn't anybody be troubled by these predictions? What will Jesus do while he is away? When will he come back? How? How can the disciples know something that they don't think that they know? Is Jesus being preposterous in his expectations? Why is he trying to comfort them? Is he placating them—or is this for real? What kind of "place" is he promising? Oddly, these questions point to truths still important today.

Question 2. If your group has raised some of the questions above, people will quickly see how troubled these disciples must feel and the many reasons they have to feel troubled. If you want a more personal question as a follow-up, consider asking, "When do you need to hear these same simple words from Jesus?"

Question 3. Study the dialogue between Jesus and Peter in 13:36-38. Notice Jesus' terse yet detailed response to each as you look for both reassurance and warning. Notice that this brief dialogue is the background for all of Jesus' teachings in chapters 14—17, sometimes called "Jesus' Farewell Address." Even though Jesus' answer to Peter is quick here, most of what he says throughout the next three chapters is a response to the questions that Peter began, later followed by similar questions from Thomas and Philip (14:5, 8).

Question 5. Nothing would be more incongruous to a first-century mind than mixing the words *crucify* and *glorify*. Crucifixion was a gory, ignoble, slow public execution reserved for criminals of the worst sort. Yet Jesus puts these two concepts side by side throughout this sermon as he helps his disciples prepare for upcoming events. (See also Jn 12:23-24, 27-33.) People familiar with the big picture of God's plan for redeeming people from their sins and drawing them to himself will enjoy the "glory" Jesus describes here far more than his disciples could have at the time. This exercise in hindsight will help us to see that even the most dismal portions of our lives may also have some larger

purpose in God's cosmic plan that we cannot yet comprehend.
Question 6. For those of us participating in this scene from the vantage point of two thousand years of Christianity, we might well wonder what is "new" about the command to love one another. Even the disciples gathered around the table would have been familiar with Leviticus 19 where, embedded with such other commands as "Do not plant your field with two kinds of seed" (v. 19), we also read, "love your neighbor as yourself" (v. 18), which Jesus quoted as the second part of the "great commandment" (see Mk 12:29-31 and Mt 22:37-40). What is new about the love commandment he now gives is the "one another" aspect. Jesus now says that this love-bond between Christ-followers would be the single greatest signal of their connection to him. The "as I have loved you" aspect of this love would soon be lived out in Christ's death and resurrection—for them. Later in 1 Corinthians 13, the apostle Paul more fully defines the kind of love the people of God are to extend to one another. This background information may contribute to a more complete discussion of the "why" aspect of question 6, as well as questions 7-10.
Question 11. Encourage self-examination and honesty (but not gossip) as people in your group discuss how they can collectively or individually contribute to an atmosphere of Christ-following love among their local body of believers.

Study 2. Which Way to God? John 14:5-14.
Purpose: To adequately apprehend Jesus' "I am the way . . ." statement and to respond accordingly.
Question 1. Throughout this entire text Jesus interweaves himself with the Father: "No one comes to the Father except through me" (v. 6); "If you really knew me, you would know my Father as well" (v. 7); "Anyone who has seen me has seen the Father (v. 9); "I am in the Father, and . . . the Father is in me" (v. 10); "the Father, living in me" (v. 10); "I am going to the Father" (v. 12); "so that the Son may bring glory to the Father" (v. 13). Notice not only these quotes, but begin to define links between the Father and Son described by them.
Question 2. Connections between these two queries are not obvious, yet both express an uncertainty about the future, and Philip's request builds on the way Jesus answered Thomas' question. Their questions also seem to reveal that they've missed Jesus' connections to the Father. Peter and Thomas reveal the finiteness of their minds—their lack of knowledge and understanding (e.g., about where Jesus is going, how to get there and

what the Father looks like)—even though they've been with Jesus for much of his ministry.

Question 3. As you look at implications of this bold statement, consider also what impact these words might have on the future of the disciples—if they fully believe that *no one* can come to the Father except through Jesus.

Question 4. Follow-up questions might include: Why do you think Jesus said this? Why do you think John wrote it? What impact would this statement have on the future of Christianity?

Question 5. With the tight links that Jesus draws here between himself and the Father, we see a beginning description of Trinity, its nature and form. Not surprisingly, the very next paragraph introduces the Spirit. Since Jesus, in his human form, would soon be leaving his disciples, it would be of great value to them (and to us) to better understand the nature of God as triune: Father, Son, and Spirit, one God yet three, threefold, yet one, trinity and unity. Probably Jesus' disciples did not fully understand (nor do we), but his explanation here gets them a start on it.

Question 6. Potential follow-up questions include: How can you meet your obligations this coming week and do what Jesus had been doing or in the way Jesus would do them? Do you need to change your plans and, if so, how and why?

Question 7. Providing spiritual redemption through death and then resurrection is, of course, beyond the scope of mere humans who follow Christ. Yet the magnitude of preaching, teaching, ministries of healing and kindness done throughout the centuries by Christ-followers in his name might constitute the "greater things" Jesus foretells of his followers. This word from Jesus that his teachings and ministry would not end when he died and then ascended must have given great hope to his bereft disciples.

Question 8. Try this experiment. We're all human; no need to try to camouflage a first reaction.

Question 9. Notice the meaning of restrictions in this statement which some would call preposterous. Note that it verifies Jesus' connection with the Father because any request that we ask (which Jesus will grant) must bring "glory" to the Father. The key phrase "so that" points out this condition. We are also told that we must ask in the name of Jesus. While many of us rightly end our prayers by saying something like "in the name of Jesus," we must be aware that praying in the name of Jesus is not a mere mouthing of those words as if they are some magical formula.

If we are to rightly pray in Jesus' name, we must ask what he would ask; our goals and motives must be in line with his. We can even ask that he will align our desires with his (which may change what we ask for) and therefore make us effective practitioners of prayer.

Question 10. Most Christians will have friends and acquaintances attempting to find other paths to God. Christians might want to exercise the kindness of confrontation to these friends by pointing out the exclusive claims of Christ. You could do a bit of role playing here to help each other think of possible responses to nonbelievers in conversations about Jesus. Or you might have people share about actual conversations they've had with nonbelievers about Jesus, and what they said. If Jesus is indeed the only way, other paths are not merely interesting; they are dangerous.

Study 3. Looking Within. John 14:15-31.
Purpose: To examine ourselves by looking within for evidence of the presence of Christ.
Question 1. Use this question to help each person in a group connect personally with a portion of the text to be studied.
Question 2. Look specifically at verses 16, 17 and 26; you'll find information about the nature and work of God's Spirit in each.
Question 3. You will find additional links between Father and Son in verses 16, 20, 21, 23, 24, 26, 28 and 31.
Question 4. If you are leading a group, encourage each person to comment on where they see themselves in this network of connections. After the discussion, pause to pray. You could ask any who are willing to speak aloud a one-sentence prayer to God, praying several times if they wish. You could then ask the group to respond together to each sentence prayer with a unison "Thank you, Lord." Or you could simply pause for several minutes of silent meditation and prayer, then close with a voiced prayer of your own at the end.
Question 5. The words *love* and *obedience* are linked in verses 15, 21 and 23. Use the information here and throughout the passage as you further define their relationship.
Question 6. By looking at the context of Jesus' reassuring statement, we find at least three possible meanings of Jesus' promise, "I will come to you." Merrill Tenney wrote, "It may be regarded as a promise of the appearances after the resurrection; or it may refer to the coming of Jesus in the person of the Holy Spirit; or it may be prophetic of the second com-

ing." Tenney prefers Jesus' postresurrection appearances as the primary meaning because of the parallel of this text with a later section of Jesus' talk recorded in John 16:16-22 (*John: The Gospel of Belief: An Analytical Study of the Text* [1946; reprint, Grand Rapids: Eerdmans, 1976], pp. 220-21). Donald Guthrie, writing in *New Bible Commentary* (Downers Grove, Ill.: InterVarsity Press, 1994), agrees that Jesus most likely meant for his disciples to look forward to seeing him after his death and resurrection three days later, but Guthrie also finds support in the text for a Pentecost interpretation. "Since the Spirit was given when Jesus was glorified, it is clear that there is a close relation between the two interpretations. This is supported by the reference to life in v. 19. A further consequence is the mutual indwelling mentioned in v. 20, which can come only through the work of the Spirit" (p. 1055). It seems possible that Jesus meant for his disciples (and us, his later followers) to find courage in all three meanings as they became more fully understood. His disciples of that night would take courage a few days later when they saw their risen Lord. Six weeks later when the Holy Spirit descended upon them and in power, they might find a larger meaning in his promise, "I will come to you." And those of us who follow Christ in our current era, with the prophecies of John's book of Revelation in our frame, will observe these first two meanings, but also look forward to Christ's personal return as we also remember his words, "I will come to you."

Question 7. In an era when people look within themselves to find almost anything—including God—many people assume that God is within them. Yet Jesus points to several conditions that testify of God's presence. For example: love and obedience to God (vv. 15, 23), knowledge of God (v. 17), the Spirit helping us remember teachings of Christ (v. 26), a sense of being "at home" in the presence of God (v. 23), peace (v. 27). For Christ-followers, these evidences are reassuring, frequent reminders of the presence of Christ within. But for those not yet belonging to him, the absence of these evidences is a cause for alarm—and repentance. If your group is composed of both believers and unbelievers, allow John's recorded evidences of Christ's presence in a life to reveal any unwarranted assumptions.

Question 8. Jesus expresses concern for disciples throughout this text, but not just for their own peace and comfortable life. Note also his concern for the world in verse 31 which hints something of his purpose in strengthening his disciples through and beyond the time of his death. In response to the question of Judas in verse 22, Jesus states a dual purpose:

"I have told you now before it happens, *so that* when it does happen you will believe" (v. 29) quickly followed by "but the world must learn . . ." (v. 31). Even then Jesus was preparing his disciples (and us, his later followers) for mission.

Study 4. Being Connected. John 15:1-17.
Purpose: To appreciate the complexity of Jesus' image of vine and branches as we strengthen our own connections within that system.
Question 1. Use this question to survey all of verses 1-17 and to connect them back to previous sections of Jesus' continued conversation. Your group should notice the familiar "love and obey" theme presented in 14:15, 23 and now developed more fully in 15:9-17. They will notice the continued invitation to pray begun in the "I will do whatever you ask in my name" of 14:13, now continued and enlarged in 15:7-8 and 16. New ideas in chapter 15 include the metaphor of the vine, the repeated concept of "remain," and a strong emphasis on love for one another as an extension of love for Christ and a deliberate patterning of the love that God the Father and God the Son share. There is also the interesting concept of God's joy (15:11), of who chose whom (15:16), and another image: that of servant and friend (15:13-15). Most of these concepts will be developed further by using the discussion questions, but this question can help your group see the breadth of what lies ahead in the study.
Question 2. Lead a detailed analysis of verses 1-8 and discuss implications of all that you find.
Question 3. There is much to encourage and also to warn any reader of this text. Among the encouragements we find that our connection to the vine allows us to bear fruit, that it is the Father (the gardener) who prunes with his kindly purpose that we will be even more faithful. We are also given (again) assurance of great power in prayer—perhaps more power than we would want. But cautions also sprinkle this text, some of them alarming. The most troubling is probably verse 6: "If anyone does not remain in me . . . such branches are . . . thrown into the fire and burned." This text provides much fodder for biblical scholars who attempt to reconcile the dark picture here with the whole sweep of biblical teaching on the permanence or temporary nature of God's gift of salvation—and on what it means to "remain." James Montgomery Boice looks at three possible views: Christians may fall away and spend eternity in hell—which he rejects. The Christians Jesus describes are merely nominal (casual) Christians who have made no real commitment and

therefore are only loosely attached to the vine and are unfruitful—which he also rejects because of various phrasings of the original language in the text. A third view, which Boice accepts, is that it is the *works* of these Christians that are burned, because their accomplishments are not the spiritual fruit that God desires. In support of this interpretation, Boice notes the shift from singular to plural, where the verse begins, "if *anyone* does not remain in me" to the plural, "such *branches are* picked up, thrown into the fire and burned" (v. 6) (*The Gospel of John: An Expositional Commentary* [Grand Rapids: Zondervan, 1978], 4:236-40).

D. A. Carson takes another view of the same text. He says, "The question must be squarely faced: can true believers lose their salvation, or not? Can a person be a branch in the vine, and then subsequently be cast off and destroyed? . . . A genuine resolution of this problem will begin with the recognition that our theology of conversion is probably inadequate. . . . True conversion in the Scriptures presupposes some genuine change in what a man truly is; but this does not stop the biblical writers from dealing with what a man says and does. Only God can assess the heart; you and I are left to assess words and deeds. . . . [Carson then refers to Jesus' parable of the four soils in Mark 4] . . . In short, genuine conversion is not measured by the hasty decision but by the long-range fruitfulness. . . . True faith holds fast till the end" (*The Farewell Discourse and Final Prayer of Jesus: An Exposition of John 14-17* [Grand Rapids: Baker, 1980], pp. 96-98).

F. F. Bruce connects Jesus' words here with the teachings of the prophet Ezekiel in his description of Israel as a useless vine in 15:1-8, but without much interpretation regarding the nature of salvation as defined in the John text (*The Gospel of John: Introduction, Exposition and Notes* [Grand Rapids: Eerdmans, 1983], p. 309).

While these are important questions of interpretation, most lifelong Christians will have already come to favor one or the other of these views of salvation—and the biblical/theological backing for it. In group discussion, it is probably wise to acknowledge these differences and the valid scholarship behind each, then move on to the personal implications of the various warnings and encouragements here. For those interested in further study, the three authors cited above (and many others) will provide much substance.

Question 6. This question will help survey the remaining half of this passage. In a walk-thru-the-text, you will notice a reprise of the link between love and obedience, this time with the Son obeying the Father as the setting for Jesus expecting his human followers to obey him. Notice also the link between love and joy and that God himself experiences joy—in us (vv. 11-12), and the sacrificial aspect of love (v. 13)—as well as the closing emphasis on love at the end of this section of text.

Question 9. Draw attention to the various pieces of information throughout verses 13-16. In addition to other privileges note the repeated promise of effective prayer. Like previous similar statements in John 14, this promise also has a condition, this time Jesus says his disciples must "ask in my name" which implies a request within Christ's nature, as though he himself were asking his Father for this gift. Nevertheless friendship with Jesus does include the privilege of effective prayer. Since our friend Jesus through his teachings and the Holy Spirit through his indwelling makes known to us the mind of the Father, we are more likely to pray what God already wants to give.

Question 11. If people have trouble responding to this question, ask them to consider what the vine and its various connections/missions would look like with the presence (or absence) of love. Most Christians will have experienced both scenarios in their relationships or ministry. Connection without love is a painful experience!

Question 12. You will find further development on the importance of love by reading John's first letter near the end of New Testament. Legend says that John was the latest of the disciples to die and that he did so with the repeated words "love one another" on his lips.

Study 5. Overcoming Rejection. John 15:18—16:16.

Purpose: To expect hardship for the cause of Christ—and to carry his message anyway.

Question 1. Use this question to survey the passage. You'll find hardships implied throughout including those described in 15:18, 20, 27; 16:1, 2, 6, 8, 16.

Question 2. Continue your survey of the text with this follow-up question. Jesus explained reasons for this rejection at each junction. See especially 15:18, 19, 20, 21, 25; 16:2, 3. Begin to consider how proponents of this new faith might look to those outside that belief system. Consider also a cosmic conflict between good and evil—Christ and Satan.

Question 4. If your group has trouble understanding the dilemma of this statement ask questions of implication such as: Does this mean that the world would have been not guilty if Jesus had not come? And by extension that today's uninformed are better off without knowing of Jesus? As you consider various options, people in your group may come to conclusions similar to scholars Merrill C. Tenney or D. A. Carson or F. F. Bruce. If not, refer to the quotations below: "The words and deeds of Christ showed by contrast how evil men can become. His presence made their sin deliberate and inexcusable. Ignorance could no longer palliate their guilt. As was stated in 3:19, 'Men loved darkness rather than light; for their works were evil.' . . . If Jesus is the Son of God, as this Gospel declares Him to be, then rejection of Him is the greatest and most fatal sin of all. Such sin is the product of an ingrained distaste for righteousness. It is the deliberate refusal of God's will. It cannot be attributed to ignorance only, or to misfortune, or to fate, or to any one of a thousand reasons by which men excuse their behavior; for Christ is self-authenticating, and those who reject Him do so because they do not want Him" (Merrill C. Tenney, *John: The Gospel of Belief: An Analytic Study of the Text* [1948; reprint, Grand Rapids: Eerdmans, 1976], pp. 232, 236).

"If hatred which his disciples were to receive from 'the world' was due to its hatred of him (verses 18, 19), the hatred which he himself received is traced back by him to hatred of God: 'they have both seen and hated me and my Father.' They saw the Father in the Son (cf. John 14:9) but did not realize that this was so. Had they recognized Jesus as the Son of God, they would have recognized the Father in him; as it was, in repudiating the Son they repudiated the Father also (cf. John 5:23b). He had come to show them the love of God, but they reacted to his love with hatred, just as, when he came to them as the light of the world, they chose darkness rather than light (John 3:19). They thus passed judgment on themselves: if they rejected the giver of true life, they shut themselves up to the only alternative—death" (F. F. Bruce, *The Gospel of John: Introduction, Exposition and Notes* [Grand Rapids: Eerdmans, 1983], p. 314).

"Jesus is not by these verses saying that men would have been totally innocent if he had not come and spoken to them and preformed his miracles. . . . The 'world' to which Jesus comes in the Gospel of John is already a sinful and rebellious world before he arrives on the scene. . . . Because Jesus has come, the world does not become sinful; rather, it is robbed of all excuses for its sin. This suggests the world was thoroughly sinful *before* Jesus came. . . . The sin they are guilty of is the sin of not knowing God even when God reveals himself most spectacularly and explicitly in Jesus Christ for the world rejects this revelation of God, and the rejection turns to persecution and hatred" (D. A. Carson, *The Farewell Discourse and Final Prayer of Jesus: An Ex-*

position of John 14-17 [Grand Rapids: Baker, 1980], pp. 120-21).
Question 6. In a culture where Christianity is popular, Christians may not experience the harsh treatment Jesus predicted. These Christians enjoy the blessings and protection of a vast company of fellow believers and a culture that, to some extent, follows the teachings of Jesus. For this they can thank God. But such a benign environment carries its own risks. These protected people must ask:

• Am I a true believer in Jesus—or am I just following the path of least resistance?

• Am I actively looking for points of tension between Christ's teachings and popular opinion so that I will remain faithful even in those pressured areas?

• Am I organizing my life in such a way that I have regular contact with unbelievers—so that I can share with them my faith in Jesus?

Question 7. Notice and interpret the help described in 16:7, 8, 11, 13, 14, 15, and even the promise of verse 16.

Note on 16:5: Both Thomas and Peter had earlier asked Jesus where he was going (13:36; 14:5). By now, however, they "are filled with grief" and no longer asking. What they need now is comfort—which Jesus provides.

Note on 16:11: The phrase "prince of this world" refers to Satan and hints at the cosmic battle between Christ and Satan as these first Christ-followers enter their mission to a hostile world.

Question 8. A person coming to Christ for salvation must overcome a number of hurdles. One of these is admitting need. Conviction of sin, righteousness and judgment, while unpleasant, brings awareness of need—for Christ. In order to choose sides, we must clearly see the alternatives.

Question 10. Jesus said in 15:19, "I have chosen you out of the world" which sets those who respond to this call in direct conflict with "the prince of the world" described in 16:11. Even today's followers of Jesus must accept the possibility of rejection by people important to us. We can also support in prayer and funds and in hands-on help those who serve in places hostile to Christianity. We need to maintain awareness of the forces of evil, and that our mission is of eternal significance. And even though we can expect occasional rejection by forces outside the faith, we should be careful not to create our own discord—particularly among brother and sister Christ-followers. Use this question to move toward practical and specific plans of action as you and others enter the fray carrying outward the message of Christ.

Study 6. Anticipating the Future. John 16:16-33.
Purpose: To plan for our future in an atmosphere of the continued power of Christ.
Question 1. Use this question to walk through the text looking for information and implications as you note the various moods and the events and words that set those moods.
Question 2. James Boice, in analyzing this section of text, speaks of three blendings of eras when Jesus says, "In a little while you will see me no more, and then after a little while you will see me" (v. 16). "First it can refer to the death of the Lord Jesus Christ and the days of His entombment, during which He was not seen, and then the Resurrection which follows with its renewed sight of Him. Second, it can indicate the periods before and after Pentecost, for now, because of the ministry of the Holy Spirit, we see Him in a spiritual way which was not possible previously. . . . Finally, it may describe the church age, this short time in which we do not see Christ with our physical eyes, but after which, when the Lord will return in glory, we shall see Him face to face and have earth's sorrows transmuted into eternal joy" (*Gospel of John,* 4:303). The joy of verse 22 might well fit into any of those three eras, indeed all three of them.
Question 4. Christian joy does not preclude sadness. Indeed joy includes sorrow and eventually supercedes it. It is entirely possible to be joyful even through tears. Joy comes from a confidence not in self or in circumstances, but in God. Joy includes an ability to "enjoy" though is not limited to joyful feelings. Sometimes feelings of joy are impossible in today's era because of circumstances or because of physical depression. Yet even then, God's people can look forward to their eternal joy in his presence and so, even in the dark, look forward to joy in a forever future.
Question 5. Jesus uses childbirth as an apt illustration of the pain and the joy ahead. Their near future included the pain of the cross and of failure in themselves. But they would also see the birth of a new relationship between God and humans and the birth of the church—in which they would fully partake.
Question 6. Review and compare John 14:13; 15:7, 16; 16:23-24. We cannot ignore this four-times-repeated promise of powerful prayer, the repetition obviously signaling its importance. Rudolf Bultmann comments:

"What is new here, in contrast to [the previous three mentions of prayer] is the emphatic statement that Jesus does not need to ask the Father to answer the prayers. Of course this does not mean that the believer is to stand in a direct relationship to God and no longer requires the mediation of Jesus. The direct relationship to God is explicitly denied in 14.8f., and prayer is made by invocation of Jesus. Rather the words . . . are intended to point out the full significance of this newly disclosed possibility of prayer: the disciples have, as it were, stepped alongside Jesus, or even taken his place: . . . As the Father loves the Son (3.35; 5.20), so he loves the believers too, and indeed, as was said in 17.23; 26, with the same love with which he loved *him*. . . . The words imply that the disciples represent him in the world and thereby participate in his honour, the honour of being loved by the Father; and the sign that this is so is their prayer. It is, so to speak, the prayer of Jesus himself; but only in that it is a prayer 'in his name.' . . . They are what they are only in virtue of their relationship to him, i.e. only because they believe in him as the Revealer of God" (*The Gospel of John: A Commentary,* ed. R. W. N. Hoare and J. K. Riches, trans. G. R. Beasley-Murray [Philadelphia: Westminster Press, 1971], pp. 588-89).

Question 7. If you are in a group, picture and describe one or two scenes for the benefit of others in the group. If you are alone in your study, sketch or write your response and pray over what this illustrative exercise reveals.

Question 8. As clarifying questions, consider asking: What did they believe (vv. 29-30)? What was going to happen in the next few days that would challenge their belief in Jesus and in themselves (vv. 31-32)?

Question 10. In a group context, ask each person to consider their near, far or eternal future and speak to the impact of verse 33 on this segment of their future.

Study 7. Defining Purpose. John 17:1-19.

Purpose: To continue the mission of Christ's disciples as we define our own purpose on earth.

Question 1. This dense prayer of only five verses reveals much of Jesus' nature and mission. Find information in every verse, and so get a glimpse of God's grand design through the earthly ministry of his Son.

Question 2. Time-related phrases in this passage include: "the time has come," "eternal life," "before the world began," "now," "completing." Use these phrases to try to understand what God reveals here about himself, about you and about your place (and his) in the universe.

Question 4. Spend an appropriate amount of time on this question as you mentally enter the first-century world and begin to comprehend the wide-reaching implications of Jesus' prayer, and the far-reaching responsibility these first disciples carried.

If you are mystified about the names of the disciples listed here and wonder why "Judas" (not Judas Iscariot) is part of the conversation with disciples in John 14:22, a little commentary work may help. The Judas of John 14 is a biblical mystery. Nothing is known about him except his name and that his father's name was James. Some think this Judas was the same person as the disciple Thaddaeus who is unmentioned in lists of disciples whenever this Judas is present. Compare Matthew 10:2-4, Mark 3:13-19, Luke 6:12-16, and Acts 1:13.

Question 8. Each of these three statements carries great impact and is worthy of prayerful contemplation. Focus long enough on each of the three statements to garner some of the spiritual meaning they reveal. The last statement may need clarification. Here F. F. Bruce is helpful:

> If the disciples are to be effectively set apart [sanctified] for the work which they must do, the Son must first set himself apart for the work which *he* must do. He therefore consecrates himself to God on their behalf: Chrysostom paraphrases "I sanctify myself" as "I offer myself in sacrifice". Here is a Johannine counterpart to the Gethsamane prayer. . . .
>
> It was not what Jesus' executioners did to him, but what he did himself in his self-offering, that makes his death a prevailing sacrifice "for the life of the world" (John 6:51; cf. 1:29). Here, then, the priest dedicates the sacrificial victim: it is because priest and victim are one that the sacrifice is not only completely voluntary but uniquely efficacious. (*The Gospel of John: Introduction, Exposition and Notes* [Grand Rapids: Eerdmans, 1983], pp. 334-35.)

Question 9. As you work with this question, consider events and teachings whereby Jesus helped people to better know his Father. Examples might include God's moral code in the Sermon on the Mount, God's tenderness as Jesus blessed the children, his compassion when Jesus helped the bleeding woman. For more ideas, page backward through any of the Gospels. Remember that Jesus said, "I and the Father are one" (John 10:30).

Question 11. Some people are constantly aware that others follow their words and example; they are natural leaders. Others, however, lead people in more subtle ways—even unconsciously. A store clerk sets the tone of a transaction by her eye contact and tone of voice. A babysitter shapes the atmosphere of a child's evening by the way he handles an accidental spill. A senior basketball player leads a freshman to play better (or worse) with mere gestures and tone of voice. All of us are leaders—to someone. With that in mind, consider the challenge of question eleven.

Study 8. Leaving a Legacy. John 17:20-26.
Purpose: To find our place in Jesus' prayer for his disciples.
Question 2. Study all four mentions of love and how that love connects Jesus to the Father and to his followers, and connects the followers with one another. Consider characteristics of love with this kind of effect.
Question 3. The sweep of this prayer is enormous: from "before the creation of the world" (v. 25) to our current age—and beyond. From the road to Gethsemane to the farthest reaches of the world (v. 21).
Question 4. Jesus' prayer describes unity between Jesus and the Father, unity between the Triune God and his people, unity between God's people with one another. Begin to think how these various unities relate to one another, and the characteristics of this kind of unity.
Question 8. The words *that* and *so that* often signal a purpose statement, and you will find several of these in the text: "so that the world may believe" (v. 21), "that they may be one as we are one" (v. 22), "to let the world know" (v. 23), "to be with me where I am" (v. 24), "to see my glory" (v. 24), "in order that the love you have for me may be in them" (v. 26). It will become apparent that many of the gifts proceeding from this prayer come with a purpose and even a responsibility.
Question 9. Make your responses as specific as possible. Consider your potential role to create unity in a church, fellowship group or family or between Christians from various cultures and distances.

J. I. Packer is Board of Governors Professor of Theology at Regent College in Vancouver, British Columbia. He also serves as contributing editor to Christianity Today. *He has authored many books, including* Knowing God. *Carolyn Nystrom is a freelance writer based in the western Chicago suburbs. She has written more than seventy-five books and Bible study guides and served as general editor for the Christian Classics series. Together they have authored several books including* Never Beyond Hope *and* Praying.

What Should We Study Next?

A good place to continue your study of Scripture would be with a book study. Many groups begin with a Gospel such as *Mark* (20 studies by Jim Hoover) or *John* (26 studies by Douglas Connelly). These guides are divided into two parts so that if twenty or twenty-six weeks seems like too much to do at once, the group can feel free to do half and take a break with another topic. Later you might want to come back to it. You might prefer to try a shorter letter. *Philippians* (9 studies by Donald Baker), *Ephesians* (11 studies by Andrew T. and Phyllis J. Le Peau) and *1 & 2 Timothy and Titus* (11 studies by Pete Sommer) are good options. If you want to vary your reading with an Old Testament book, consider *Ecclesiastes* (12 studies by Bill and Teresa Syrios) for a challenging and exciting study.

There are a number of interesting topical LifeGuide studies as well. Here are some options for filling three or four quarters of a year:

Basic Discipleship
Christian Beliefs, 12 studies by Stephen D. Eyre
Christian Character, 12 studies by Andrea Sterk & Peter Scazzero
Christian Disciplines, 12 studies by Andrea Sterk & Peter Scazzero
Evangelism, 12 studies by Rebecca Pippert & Ruth Siemens

Building Community
Fruit of the Spirit, 9 studies by Hazel Offner
Spiritual Gifts, 8 studies by R. Paul Stevens
Christian Community, 10 studies by Rob Suggs

Character Studies
David, 12 studies by Jack Kuhatschek
New Testament Characters, 10 studies by Carolyn Nystrom
Old Testament Characters, 12 studies by Peter Scazzero
Women of the Old Testament, 12 studies by Gladys Hunt

The Trinity
Meeting God, 12 studies by J. I. Packer
Meeting Jesus, 13 studies by Leighton Ford
Meeting the Spirit, 10 studies by Douglas Connelly